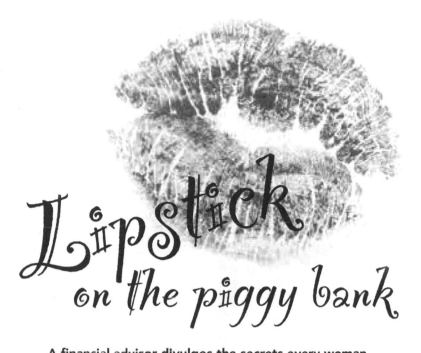

Lipstick
on the piggy bank

A financial advisor divulges the secrets every woman
should know about happiness, money and independence.

Nicole N. Middendorf, CDFA

BEAVER'S
POND
PRESS

ISBN 13: 978-1-59298-566-1

Library of Congress Catalog Number: 2012918734

Printed in the United States of America

First Printing: 2013

17 16 15 14 13   5 4 3 2 1

Cover design by Alan Wallner owner W Creative
Interior design and typesetting by James Monroe Design, LLC.

Beaver's Pond Press
7108 Ohms Lane
Edina, MN 55439–2129
952-829-8818
www.BeaversPondPress.com

To order, visit www.BeaversPondBooks.com or call 1-800-901-3480.
Reseller discounts available.

Contents

Acknowledgements

I owe so much to my family and my friends and my staff. Thank you so much for being there for me.

Everyone in my office...you all amaze me!! Thank you for all that you do everyday and what you do to make a difference in my life and the lives of others.

To Natalie, thank you so much for making my life easier and loving my kids and helping me to be a great mom.

Thank you Deb, my therapist, who encouraged me and helped to keep me focused during those difficult times.

Thank you to everyone that was involved in this project. Your guidance and support mean everything to me.

Clients, thank you for allowing me the opportunity to help you achieve your dreams and have financial happiness.

Thank you Mom and Dad. Your endless love means the world to me. Thank you for always being there for me when I needed you most.

Thank you to those of you that made an impact in my life over the years and helped me see the true value of life and happiness. May you achieve all that you dream (and of course a few items on your bucket list).

This book is dedicated to my two children, Parker and Gabrielle. Thank you so much for being an inspiration to me. Thank you for your unconditional love. I wish you both all the happiness in the world and to understand that money truly doesn't bring happiness.

With Happiness,
Nicole N. Middendorf, CDFA
LPL Financial Advisor
CEO Prosperwell Financial
www.prosperwell.com

The opinions voiced in this material are for general information only and are not intended to provide specific advice or recommendations for any individual. To determine which investment(s) may be appropriate for you, consult your financial advisor prior to investing. All performance referenced is historical and is no guarantee of future results. All indices are unmanaged and cannot be invested into directly.

Introduction

I wanted to write a book to help women with money. I feel too many women are taken advantage of and I wanted a resource to help empower women with their finances and futures.

When I learned that one in four women are in an abusive relationship, I knew I could do something about it. Reading books is what kept me going through those dark times. I created a resource to help women so we could change the landscape of financial literacy.

If nothing else, know that single most important thing is to believe there is never a dumb question when it comes to money. There is a stigma around asking for help and you and me can abolish it, creating women who are passionate and empowered about their futures. I am so proud of being a financial advisor and helping my clients make their dreams come true.

This is to all women in all life's situations. You can do it!

*For confidentiality, names have been changed where appropriate.

Women, Money and Happiness

"I wanted a perfect ending. Now I've learned, the hard way, that some poems don't rhyme, and some stories don't have a clear beginning, middle and end. Life is about not knowing, having to change, taking the moment and making the best of it, without knowing what's going to happen next. Delicious Ambiguity."

—GILDA RADNER

Achieving True Happiness: The Myth of Being Rich

We live in a society that values money more than happiness. According to the World Values Survey in 2005, Americans took thirteenth place in the top 50 for achieving true happiness. This is a staggering contrast to what we see played out on reality television, national media reports and women's magazines. During 2010, Gallup released their world poll that surveyed over 155 countries between 2005 and 2009[1].

---

1. http://www.forbes.com/2010/07/14/
    world-happiest-countries-lifestyle-realestate-gallup.html

1

What the researchers were seeking was far more difficult than they imagined. Could they prove a "rich" country was happier than a "poor" country? In this study, the United States ranked fourteenth for happiness. Of those that responded to the study, 57 percent indicated they were "thriving." But no single report can truly tell us how happy we are, and this is an important factor in the happiness equation. Of course researchers and analysts can't measure happiness—in our daily lives, most of us aren't even sure if we are truly happy.

I want you to take out a pen and a piece of paper. Draw a line down the middle and divide the page into two separate sections. Write "I was happy when..." in the left column and finish the sentence. Now write "I would be happy if..." in the right column. I'd like you to sit for a few moments and take in those words.

I was happy when.... I would be happy if....

These are the same words we mutter daily as we try to conquer the feelings of internal happiness and struggle. These words will not pave the way to enlightenment or future bliss. The more we speak these words internally, the more we chip away at the belief that we can be happy. When you're ready, make a promise to yourself that the "ifs" and "whens" of your happiness will no longer rule your life. The "I was happy whens" and "I would be happy ifs" are no longer allowed to rule your speech or your psyche. Instead of the "if" and "when," consider saying, "I am happy now because..." Simply finding ONE positive thing can change your entire outlook.

The Influence of Media

One of the biggest perpetuators of unhappiness is today's media. The media tries to portray the happiness of women as both simplistic and difficult to attain. In commercials, sitcoms and movies we see ourselves BUYING things to fill a void, all while questioning our worth, beauty or power. If happiness was as simplistic as buying the right fabric softener, going to the best gym and wearing only designer labels, we wouldn't be happy as much as boring and similar.

Marketers, ad agencies and the companies they represent don't want you to know that happiness is a choice. They want you to see a glimmer of hope on a page in a magazine or a commercial and instantly want to be THAT woman. The fact of the matter is, it works. Not only does it work, it works too well. While this book isn't about debunking the myths and lies told to women by companies and advertisements, it is about seeing through the words and emotions pushed on us daily and making smart financial decisions that will lead to real, long-term happiness.

Look at what our culture teaches us. How many daily messages to spend money do we get? Moreover, to spend money in order to be happy? No alternative or inspirational messages get the amount of airtime that commercials and reality television do. How many messages tell you to save your money rather than spend it?

To be a saver means going against the grain of societal pressure. The sad truth is buying the bigger house and the fancier car won't bring you happiness. I recently talked about the "ifs" and "whens" of being happy with my friend Deb, the owner of Connected and Committed[2]. When we sat down

---

2. www.connectedandcommitted.com

and discussed our old ideas of being happy, she said, "I once thought that when I purchased my leather couch, *that'll be it*. I had it delivered, and sat on it and thought, *that was it*? [I thought that happiness meant that] anything I ever bought was going to deliver what they promised it would." She said that on looking back, the idea that a leather couch could fulfill her greatest desire now makes her laugh.

Through her years in counseling others about relationships and helping women establish healthy patterns and boundaries, Deb discovered one, undisputed truth. She looked at me and told me her secret to unhappiness: "We are afraid to be good to ourselves." Often we think that "being good to ourselves" means buying a new handbag or getting a more expensive haircut. But being truly good to ourselves—our bodies and minds—means seeing through the messages that society feeds us about jealousy and wanting more than we have. It's not wrong to work for something and savor getting it, but it is wrong to let the cultural pressure of today's world make us feel like we're owed it, or that once we attain it we'll be happy.

Self-Acceptance: Shaping Our Happiness from Within

How does our self-acceptance shape our lives? For those of us coming out of a troubled relationship with our parents, spouse, partner or ourselves, that relationship is a perfect mirror of what we buy into. We're taught to accept that the expectations of other people define us. We are so caught off guard by the realization that we DESERVE to be happy. As you'll read in Chapter 3, I emerged from a troubled marriage to find myself intact and ready to take on the world.

We all have many defining moments in our lives, and

the birth of my daughter, Gabrielle, was a major one for me. None of us are immune to the trap of wanting it all. I speak often about wanting to keep my family, marriage and home together at all costs. I didn't realize that I couldn't give myself the permission to let go. I was the only one who could give myself permission to be who I was meant to be. I always believed things happen for a reason, but I was afraid to let go of the mentality that I needed the perfect house as well.

I have come to learn that I can only control the things I have the power to control. I can't control the stock market, the government or the behavior of my friends or ex spouse. I teach my clients that we can control where we save money and how we invest. Deb once said, "When we get back in control of our feelings, we have the avenue and tools to create the life we want." She couldn't be more right.

1-Week, 6-Months, 1-Year

I'd like to share a client of mine's story with you. Anna had a very serious shopping addiction. While working at a demanding job, Anna often let off steam at the mall by picking up shoes, clothing or accessories on her way home. As we talked, it came out that there were literally dozens of shoes in Anna's closet that she never had worn and clothes still on hangers with price tags from years ago. Anna knew she was facing a defining moment: either she needed to find a way to change her behavior, or her future retirement would be at risk.

Also addicted to her Franklin Planner, I advised Anna to go ahead and buy the next pair of shoes she wanted. However, she couldn't wear them for two weeks and she would have to tuck the receipt into her Franklin Planner for 30 days.

If in 30 days she hadn't worn the shoes, she had to return them. As a result of the experiment, Anna generally returned the shoes shortly after purchasing them, realizing her pattern of spending. Instead of funding her shoe closet, we funded her future and secured a healthy outlook with the help of a therapist.

Whenever you buy something, consider how you'll feel about it and how much you'll use in it 1-week, 6-months or 1-year. As women we are often drawn to sales, and I tell clients to not buy into the savings unless the item will truly be worth the sale price. We love getting a good deal, but the shirt or jeans won't do our future much good if they sit in our closet unworn.

Trouble saying "No" when a sale calls? Take the store's sales receipt and put it 30 days ahead in your planner or journal. If you haven't worn or used the item, consider returning it like Anna did. Be empowered about smart financial solutions!

Do a weekly inventory of your purchases by keeping a journal. You might notice some trends that make you question your spending habits. Every 6 months, go through your closet. Find items to donate or to bring to consignment to sell. You'll clear out space—and guilt—by giving the unused or forgotten a new home. Yearly, set personal goals to establish better spending and saving patterns. In 1-week, 6-months and 1 year you can fund yourself to a healthier financial future.

No More Band-Aids

In the struggle to meet the demands of society, many of my clients are looking for a quick fix to solve financial problems. One of the most common Band-Aids I see is refinancing their homes. Often a refinance works like unstable glue—it will help with the immediate bills, but you will be left with a higher mortgage balance and many times, battling an upside-down mortgage.

The first question you need to ask yourself is, "How did I end up in the situation I am in?" Like Anna, you can control your future choices and habits, but it takes determination and oftentimes a financial advisor to guide you to the right solutions. One of the worst disservices we can do ourselves is to choose an easy fix that will have detrimental long-term effects. As difficult as your financial situation may be, there is always room to turn the boat around.

Cut Yourself a Check

When clients ask if they can afford a bigger house, I often advise them to write themselves a check for the difference of the new mortgage, put it in an envelope and save the money in the meantime. Do this process for 6 months. By pretending you are in the house and physically writing out the checks every month, you can decide if the amount is something you're willing to invest in.

Female Report Card:

Are the Kardashians really happy? Why don't the relationships from reality television last? The answer is simple: their lifestyles are unrealistic. Money doesn't buy happiness. As women, we are always comparing ourselves to one another and tend to focus on the consumer side of life. While there is huge pressure to spend money, I truly believe women would be much happier if they spent less. Culture creates a black hole that is very difficult to fill. There is a constant need to have more and measure up. Buying something new will not fill your black hole or give you a better grade on the report card of what you've accomplished.

Money works a lot like how a diet works. We are constantly comparing our bodies to those of women on the television or on the street. The fact of the matter is, we don't know their financial backstory, whether or not they've had surgery or if they are deeply in debt and unhappy. We diet expecting to have results that compare to how someone else looks. Sometimes, we don't take into account our bone density or the way our body processes fat and exercise. To change our lifestyle, we need to look at all the aspects of our personal situation and not compare ourselves to others.

Eliminating the Female Report Card means that we start using the right language to change our perceptions and establish good financial and self-awareness:

- **Instead of saying, "They have it all," say, "I will not buy into..."**

- **Instead of saying, "I wish I had..." say, "I do not need..."**

- **Instead of thinking, "I will never be as (beautiful/talented/rich) as..." say, "I have all the skills, self-awareness and ability to be whoever I want to be."**

The True Formula

If there is one thing above all that I have learned it is that happiness is not a recipe, nor is it a formula. For many, the happiness equation looks like this:

Loving Parents + Perfect Family + Great Education +
Popularity + Stylish Clothing + Perfect Job + Mr. Right +
Three-Story House + ... (You get the idea.)

It's absolutely overwhelming to try to plan the "perfect" life. Usually, the imperfections of our lives are exactly what make it our own and are the only things that separate us from someone else. My wish for you is to develop a pair of X-ray glasses. Each time you are mesmerized by what someone else has, be it a spouse, money, house or power, take time to look through the situation. There is one thing we always need to remember: the more someone presents the idea of a perfect life, the more I question what is really going on.

If you've ever been on an airplane, you know that the flight attendants always tell you that in case of an emergency, you'll need to put on your own oxygen mask before assisting others. Are you trying to cultivate happiness in everyone around you, but neglecting your own peace of mind? You have the right to say, "Me first" and mean it. Put on your own financial oxygen mask before assisting your children or grandchildren.

We don't know the whole story or what goes on behind the scenes. I have many clients that came to me wanting bigger houses, fancier cars or something else. I show them that true and lasting happiness doesn't come from something bigger, rather it comes from something that is affordable and will last far longer than the sparkle of something new. We spend far too much time filling our closets and far too little time planning for our success and financial future.

The idea of the perfect life is a fallacy. Someone once shared with me that we are all on a boat. The waves underneath the hull always rise and fall, like a teeter-totter. True happiness is being out of balance and still finding peace with everything around you. Instead of chasing perfection, go after a far greater goal: life-long prosperity through preparation. Looking back, you'll be far happier.

If happiness could be any sort of equation, it would be much more simple and direct:

Acceptance (of self and others) + Knowledge (that you CAN achieve what you want) = Happiness

The Top 3 Myths of (un)Happiness

1. Happiness is Money.

Women and men think they'll be happy when they finally make more money or get the next raise. They believe happiness is a milestone, but the truth is that it's far from it. When you get out of debt, something will always happen. This something is called "life." There is always something to achieve in life. Too many times, I've seen my clients and friends focused on creating monetary wealth instead of internal happiness. When we measure ourselves against our peers or those on the television, the myths of happiness become unattainable. When you add more money, more things or a spouse, kids or business, your life becomes more complicated. Happiness lies in the want to be happy and life's simple pleasures. At the end of your life, I guarantee, you would have traded each dollar left over for more time with those you love and cherish. Happiness isn't in bills or coins, it's in love and acceptance.

JoAnn's Story

JoAnn married Mark while they were both in their early twenties. Mark always spent money. In the beginning it was on music or small purchases, but they always added up. When her husband started a business several years later, JoAnn became concerned with his spending, especially after they moved into a very large home. JoAnn's friends often commented, "I wish I lived in your house." Always smiling and gracious, JoAnn thanked her friends but never revealed how truly miserable she was.

In going through their finances, JoAnn had to come to terms with some serious choices Mark had made. Although they had a large house and Mark's business, they were significantly in debt—so much so that they briefly explored the option of bankruptcy. The gorgeous home and the successful business didn't make JoAnn happy, they made her worried and anxious.

JoAnn left Mark later that year knowing that the decision was leading to an important crossroad in her life. After meeting with JoAnn and establishing a plan, it came out that although Mark was a spender, JoAnn was a saver (and she continues to be one of the smartest and most frugal people I know).

Once a shy, stay-at-home mom, JoAnn has completely changed. She now works for a company and loves her job. She continues to save and lives in a small, beautiful condo. Most importantly, she is truly satisfied with her life and choices. We decided together that it wasn't about the money, JoAnn's memories and future success were far too important to stay in a spiraling pattern.

2. Happiness is About What You Have Yet to Achieve.

If internal bliss depended on what we didn't have or couldn't possess yet, no one would be happy. You can choose what to delight in. In my life, I find happiness in possibility and my children's laughter. I have yet to meet a parent who believes that bliss occurs when their baby reaches adulthood. We find contentment in precious moments of learning and growing. As adults, we forget to afford ourselves the same benefit of believing that the depth of the good is in the here and now. We often excuse-away the moments in the present because we think the future will be so much brighter. Nothing is guaranteed and the largest disservice we can do to ourselves is to limit our possibility of being truly happy because we haven't achieved some goal we've set.

Jill and Todd's Story

Jill and Todd have been happily married for many years. Whenever they come into my office, they are holding hands and listening to each other not only in words, but in body language. When Jill expresses frustration or speaks about being uneasy, Todd grabs her hand or her shoulder and gives her the look that says, "I am here." While it's a pleasure having them in my office for that reason alone, they also have a shared goal for the future.

Jill and Todd have decided that their happiness lies in being able to help those around them by giving back. We meet regularly and discuss the causes they are drawn to and how they can give while still saving and securing their own future. They live within their means and save whenever they can. They are also well-known for their philanthropy and kindness. They have the formula down and it shows.

Jill and Todd live their life with balance. Still vacationing, eating out occasionally and making their house a home, they have no fear about the future. The question they ask most often is, "Will we be able to give more next year?" I'm proud of them and all they are accomplishing.

3. I Don't Deserve to be Happy.

There are many people I've met that live with the impression that satisfaction requires a permission slip. Clients and friends alike have expressed these sentiments to me. Their voices echo, "This wasn't how it's supposed to be. I can't be happy." Happiness is a choice. That choice begins with the realization that, if we spend our entire lives looking for acceptance from others, the only thing we're guaranteed to find is resentment within ourselves. By looking for permission or acceptance, we are buying into the belief that there is a golden ticket to happiness that we don't possess. To solve this problem, the most important question you can ask yourself is, "What can I do to be happy, NOW?" Happiness isn't a secret and it certainly doesn't involve a permission slip. The sad truth is that today's companies and marketers know that the ticket to your bliss is quite simply an attitude adjustment. You have the power to internally mute the commercials claiming that you need a new product or lifestyle to complete who you are. You don't need to hear from me that you are beautiful NOW, before you lose those 10 pounds over the next 3 months. The only thing you need to complete your wardrobe, bank account or future plans is the promise to yourself that no matter what happens, you will accept yourself as you are and know you are capable of great and amazing things.

Amy's Story

Amy went through a very troubled spot in her marriage a few years ago. Waking up each morning, Amy struggled to find the strength and determination to get through the day. Her two children were one of her only sources of happiness. Amy wanted to leave her husband, but couldn't bear the possibility of hurting the children.

Trying to justify her anger and unhappiness led to the realization that Amy needed to choose happiness immediately. Although ending her marriage was very difficult and challenged Amy with going through many steps in securing employment and a new home, she is now happier than ever. Her children are also happier to not see their parents fighting every day. However, when Amy and I first sat down to make the decision to put her happiness first, it was not an easy process. It was hard for her to see that she could not financially provide the 'perfect' life for her children, which kept Amy struggling to make the marriage work. The truth is, we don't know the length of our life. If we could be guaranteed 100 years, we might make different choices. For Amy, it was important that she secure happiness and financial freedom now, as opposed to waiting any longer. By no longer putting everyone else before herself, Amy found herself worthy of happiness and she is now determined to live her best life.

Begin Today, Find Happiness

To find happiness, we need to start from within. Happiness is an attitude. It's a choice. It is NOT a tangible item. It has to be earned from the greatest critics: ourselves. In the next few pages, you'll find a guide to starting your path to happiness. It includes focusing on a happy memory, finding a place of contentment and most importantly, learning to accept yourself.

Describe Your Happiness Memory

In describing my first moment of happiness, I'd have to go back to growing up. My parents gave me the opportunity to choose what activities I wanted to be involved in. I took dance, piano, tennis, choir, band, softball and figure skating (just to name a few). It wasn't so much the activities that brought me happiness, but the ability to choose what I wanted to do. I've always loved learning and developing. The different skills of each activity made me realize I could do much more than I first thought. It built my confidence. My parents gave me the ultimate gift in letting me expand beyond what limitations I thought I had.

> Finding your happiness memory isn't about dwelling in the past, but being content in the present. Because I was given the opportunity to choose what I wanted to learn, I make better choices now. Just like job seekers have transferrable skills, a happiness memory can be the key to what ignites you today.

Soon it was clear to me that although I enjoyed each sport and activity, I truly loved figure skating. The moment my skate hit the ice, I felt at peace. I knew I could conquer each move with precision and grace. And if I didn't conquer it right away, I would practice and practice with complete focus and determination. I learned these values and many more, all of which remain with me today. My success was a direct effect of being raised in an environment that said, "You can do this." Later in my life, as a skating coach, my students would come to me and say "I can't do it." I would tell them, "I'm sorry, but I don't know what 'can't' means." For every "can't" they used, they would pay me a dollar, which I would then return to their parents (the students didn't know this). Eventually, "can't" was no longer part of their language.

In an indirect way, the students learned what my parents had taught me. I try to live my life without mental blocks or the fear that I won't be able to accomplish something. When I have a moment of doubt, I remember that I am capable, intelligent and powerful. My happiness is knowing that I CAN do anything I put my mind and heart into, just as YOU CAN do anything that you put your mind and heart into.

The Importance of Mentors

In my job as a financial advisor, I see myself as a mentor, advisor, motivator and partner to those who want to accomplish a goal. I often ask my clients, "When was the last time you felt truly inspired by someone or something around you?" As we grow older, our need for a mentor does not decrease, it rises. Having someone to call, or listen to and encourage you is one of the greatest gifts you can give yourself. We often lose our vision or determination in the midst of difficulty.

I wouldn't be who I am today without those who have mentored me. While starting my business, I had a vision board that was truly helpful—keeping me focused on what I wanted and aligning my goals and visions for the future. You can make your own vision board by simply taking a large piece of paper, cardboard or even a frame and putting in words that describe your goals and attitude towards your future. By describing what you want to become, the words and images replace those that create negativity or anxiety. Here's a shopping list to create your own vision board:

- *1 poster board, any color*

- *1 glue stick, adhesive dots or scotch tape*

- *Clippings from various magazines, childhood photos and/or quotes and words that inspire you.*

- *2-3 uninterrupted hours. Your vision board may become a work in progress, but give yourself the opportunity to create it, kid-and phone-free. Focus on what you want to accomplish.*

Place the board in your bedroom or home office. You want to see and celebrate it daily. A vision board is also the perfect project if you have absolutely no idea what you want in your life. Keep a folder at home or at the office. Whenever you run across an article, photo or quote that inspires you and makes you think, add it to the folder. Eventually your folder will be full and you can take the items and make a vision board. Looking at what you've chosen can be eye-opening and can help you pinpoint exactly what your heart is telling you to go after.

In addition, don't forget the power of helping another person that was once in your shoes or the importance of asking for help. We are not weaker for asking for help, it's the exact opposite. I'm blessed having been mentored by not one, but many women and men I look up to for advice and counseling. After becoming involved in a mastermind group, they assisted me in making decisions that have influenced my success as a business owner and financial advisor.

Find Your Happy Place

On lazy summer afternoons, you can find me on my boat. I'm not sure if it's the flow of water underneath, being in control of where the boat goes or sitting on the water and relaxing in the sun and reading, but I know my place of contentment is on the lake. In the winter months when boating isn't possible, I have a couch in my bedroom where I relax, read, journal and cuddle with my kids. Too often, we are told that happiness happens when we spend money. Although I'm sure I could find moments of complete bliss on the beaches of Hawaii, I've learned to steal moments of happiness where I can, whether in the captain's seat or on my bedroom couch.

Many women find "happiness" in shoe shopping, but I challenge you to find it in something free or low-cost. Here's a list of three places that you just might find rewarding and fun:

1. **The Bathtub with a Few Shakes of Baking Soda.** Although I love certain scents, sometimes I want to get in the bath and read a book without having to use a $5 bath bomb. A few shakes from the cardboard baking soda box will leave your skin just as smooth, only without the fragrance. While you're in the bath, grab a book, light some candles and turn on some music or even find some items for your vision board. With the stress of our daily lives, our body and mind needs time to unwind and digest what has occurred.

2. **Open Mic Night at the Local Bookstore or Coffeehouse.** Authors, writers and musicians often share their works with others during open mic nights before they publish. You can hear a short story or a poem and support local art all at once. As humans, we have a distinct desire to be heard and acknowledged. One of the fastest ways to happiness is to try new things and expand your horizons of what you do and people you see. You may find yourself inspired by the words or the emotions of each piece.

3. **Join a Networking Group.** Along the same lines as expanding your artistic view is expanding your view of your community and its offerings. Through a networking group you may meet new friends, mentors and peers that you wouldn't have otherwise. It's also a great place to find out about volunteer opportunities, board memberships and other activities in your area. Remember, not all networking groups are created equal. Like dating, you may have to try a few before you find a great match.

Happiness Isn't in the Hoard

Have you watched Hoarders? The one time I caught the show, I couldn't help thinking of clients and friends I've known that bought items to collect that soon overwhelmed them. Be it figurines or baskets or even cosmetics,

> Don't lock yourself away in a castle. You may have a beautiful house, but a house isn't a life. We have less than 100 years to achieve everything we want. Too often we sit at home, ashamed of what we don't have. It's time to go after what we want and leave the fortress.

in the end we can't take these items with us, can we?

The same mentality goes for money. We shouldn't hoard our money, but rather invest it and get it to work for us to establish a secure future. Happiness isn't about items on a shelf, it's about security and the ability to go after what we want in any stage of our life. Shelves full of collections can't assure you financial freedom like a great plan can.

Life Situations

True happiness lies in contentment. How do we find contentment when the world is telling us otherwise? Here are three major transitions with personal stories that I hope you find filled with grace and wisdom.

Job Loss

In today's job market, the stress of keeping your job and functioning at your best is difficult. Sally recently lost her job. We met frequently to discuss her strategy of minimizing the risk of depleting her retirement while securing work. While reviewing her financials one afternoon, it came out that Sally really wanted to start a business.

Not only did she start a business, she became wildly successful. So many women I've met thought they had to work for someone else to be happy and successful. Sally knew that wasn't the case and worked very hard to live life on her terms.

Death of a Family Member or Friend

There is no pain like losing someone you cherish. I started meeting with Amanda when she was struggling to make it month-to-month. Amanda came from a troubled childhood and in a few months lost her father and ex-husband. Her ex-husband never removed Amanda as the beneficiary on his life insurance and retirement pension. Because of this, Amanda came into a great deal of money at the same time she lost her job. Although two people she cared greatly about were gone, by investing and saving both the inheritance from her father and money from her ex-husband, she was able to get out of debt and secure her future.

Amanda was given a gift that couldn't have happened otherwise. She was very particular about wanting to save as much as she could and get out of debt quickly. Sometimes, we don't know the reasons that life happens the way it does, but we can choose how to cope with it all.

Letting Go of a Troubled Relationship

Being an only child, I tend to really lean on my close friends. However, since my divorce I have become very cautious with whom I let into my life. I've learned the power in terminating a friendship and relationship both online and off. I find that people tend to reconnect with me when they are in need of something. It's a hard balance between giving and getting when those situations arise.

Recently, an old friend contacted me when she needed help with a situation. I had a difficult decision to make, suspecting that she may only be around for the advice and nothing more. I decided to talk with her to find out if she wanted a lasting friendship or a solution. Suspicions confirmed, we both decided to move forward and wish each other well. Women are socialized to help everyone around them. As a professional woman who wants to ensure that I have time for my children, my clients and most importantly, myself, I knew I made the right decision when choosing how to invest my time in this case. One of the hardest lessons I learned was that it is okay to say, "This isn't right for me, right now." There's a lot of power in those words and I am fortunate to use them. You should be too.

Make the Choice

Is choosing to be happy difficult? Happiness begins with ourselves, making the choice to see the negative and the positive and not letting them overwhelm us. My children, Parker (P.J.) and Gabrielle (Gabi) have given me new life with their imaginations. My parents bought them a John Deere Gator. Although P.J. was excited to drive around in it, they were more excited about the opportunity of a single, large box.

> Having a sense of humor is important. Too many times, people are a little too serious. Being a professional doesn't mean not having fun. As adults we need to value humor more. It's certainly helped me through major transitions.

After a year, the box is in shreds from its short life as a rocket ship, a house, a race car, a boat and so much more. Kids have so much to teach us about happiness. As adults, we forget that we don't need to spend a lot of money to have a lot of fun. What we need is the room to breathe and be creative, whatever that may be. True happiness means putting away the cell phone, enjoying the people you are with and truly engaging the environment around you. I wanted a home and I have one, but it wasn't until I dirtied my hands with painting and decorating that it felt like it belonged to me. Our choices make or break our lives. It's time to invest in happiness.

Children and Money

"Children will not remember you for the material things you provided, but for the feeling that you cherished them."
—Richard L. Evans

Our job as parents is to teach our children, even when it's inconvenient. Just as we invest our money in the stock market or bonds, we must invest our knowledge in our children. In my first book, *Simple Answers: Life is More Than Just About Money*, I wrote, "How you think, feel, spend and save your money has a correlation to how you were raised and the memories you have of money." The moral of this chapter focuses on reestablishing healthy boundaries with your children in speaking about money and teaching healthy saving patterns for their successful futures.

Children and their families come from diverse socioeconomic backgrounds. While these backgrounds have very different qualities and standards of living, the constant that grounds these extremely different realities is the value of the dollar. Children, who acquire a working knowledge of the actual value of money, learn to function and act comfortably in any environment early on. Learning basic economic principles will allow them to truly understand that possessions do not measure a person's worth or determine one's character. Economic sense equals life sense.

The Parent's Quick Survival Guide to Explaining the "Whys" of Finances

Good Money Manners

There is something about a kid with great manners. When their little mouths utter "please" or "thank you," we melt. In fact, some of us even teach our babies sign language to help them state "please" and "thank you" during and after a meal. Why on earth aren't we teaching good money manners?

Just as we educate our children to understand the basics of communication and being polite, we desperately need to educate them about financial literacy. One simple activity can change your child's perception of money. Just like encouraging our children to write thank-you notes for gifts, we should encourage them to write plans for where their financial gifts might go. When Grandma gives them $50 for their birthday, consider sitting down with them and explaining how important it is to follow my Save, Donate and Spend list:

Save = 50% Donate = 25% Spend = 25%

By teaching children the importance of breaking down money and getting comfortable saving and donating, you'll find that your child more easily accepts the ideas. Plus, as your little one grows, this is a fantastic way to teach about those less fortunate, or find a cause that speaks to their heart. Good money manners are truly a win-win!

"I Want"—Wants vs. Needs

It all begins with a simple two-word phrase: I want! A child's wants and monetary values need to be immediately distinguished from needs. This is one of the foundations of a healthy financial education! A great way to set goals is to grab a piece of paper the next time your son or daughter asks for an item or money and list it under needs or wants.

Kids truly need to recognize the difference between needs and wants. If you want to play a fun game with your family, grab one of the Sunday Target or Walmart flyers. Cut out several pictures, like toilet paper, a Barbie, toothpaste and a new video game. Have your kids paste each item under needs or wants all by themselves. Talk over each item and give positive reinforcement when the answer is correct, such as, "Yes! That video game is definitely a want." When they paste a toy item or something that truly isn't a need under the need column, explain WHY their decision might not be wise. The next time you are at a store, bring the paper with you. Have them point to items in the store and clarify whether they are needs or wants. You may find this process also helps YOU decipher between what you absolutely must have and what you can go a week without. You might be able to save enough in your budget to get one of the bigger "wants" in the future, like a vacation. We are sometimes so focused on teaching our children valuable lessons that we forget we also need an opportunity to learn once again.

"It's Only $1!"—When Cheap Still Isn't "In-Budget"

When your child asks for something, try explaining, "This toy is almost $20. That's a lot of money to save. I'm happy to help you save for it for the future, but it is out of our budget right now." By helping your child own their financial decisions, you give them respect and power to make good decisions. They might want to save their allowance or do extra chores to earn the money. Or they might forget. The next time you are at the store and they ask again, you can say, "You are almost there. So far you've saved $15! I bet by next week you can earn that toy through all your hard work. Way to go!" This gives your child a self-esteem boost and positive reinforcement for saving their money.

Don't just make this a one-time lesson. The next time you are doing bills and they ask to spend time with you, as frustrated as you are, talk them through what your monthly bills are and how you work to pay the bills. They'll see mom and dad as beacons of wisdom and they'll start to learn another piece of the financial puzzle.

"That's Not Fair!"—The Truth About Checkout Tantrums and Why They Happen

Goal-setting is an important part of our adult lives and can help our families better understand the value of each penny. I highly recommend involving your little ones in money decisions as quickly as you can, even in the most inopportune times.

Let's say you have a son or daughter that always seems to want something during checkout at the grocery store. Instead of getting frustrated time and time again, explain why they cannot have a candy bar or one of the toys. Stores bank on the fact that as parents, we'd rather avoid an argument and purchase an item than say, "No." In fact, did you ever wonder why the sugar cereals, candy and toys are always at a little one's eye-level? Stores spent an incredible amount of money on research involving children and impulse buys:

A study published in the June 2008 issue of the Journal of Consumer Research suggests that consumers are more susceptible to making impulsive purchases for one brand over another if they are distracted while shopping. In the study, Central Michigan University Psychology professor Bryan Gibson surveyed college students by measuring their preference for a variety of soft drinks, including Coke and Pepsi. Results of Gibson's study found that implicit attitudes, or those that people may not be conscious of and able to verbally express, predicted product choice only when participants were presented with a cognitive task, suggesting that implicit product attitudes may play a greater role in product choice when the consumer is distracted or making an impulse purchase.[3]

There is no distraction like a screaming toddler or a demanding 6-year-old. Impulse buying can lead to impulsive children without limits. Curb their appetite for what they don't need by explaining early and often why an item just isn't necessary.

As parents we are taught the *redirection* method—another great way to help explain why the candy or toy won't

---

3.   Study Shows Consumers May be Swayed by Distraction Newswise, Retrieved on July 16, 2008.

be purchased—that offers an alternative that you can do together in the meantime. Take this scenario: You are out with Will, your charming but often temperamental 3-year-old. Like a magnet to the refrigerator, Will's eye catches a toy next to the check-out. He picks it up, looks at you and asks if he can have it. It's time to stand your ground, Mom—use this moment to help Will understand the "Why" behind your financial decisions. The moment he raises his voice, you calmly explain, "Will, I know you are excited to bring this home, but it isn't in our budget. When we get home, maybe we can make a sticker chart and work together to find a solution. You might be able to earn that toy!" As Will tenses up, show him the value by quickly involving him in a project. "Will, can you help me count the items on the checkout belt? I bet there are more than twenty! Let's do it together." Will leaves the store with a positive money memory and you have conquered his inner checkout demon. Remember, the store is counting on you giving in to your child, rather than standing firm and teaching good money manners. You've got this!

> You are not an ATM. When your teenager asks you for money, don't hesitate to ask them to develop a real plan of how they will pay you back and hold them to it! Responsibility comes from being held accountable and needing to develop solutions for everyday problems. This might be the push your son or daughter needs to get a part-time job!

Our children are sponges for information. Every day, they watch how we interact with purchases and see our attitudes towards money. If we are constantly complaining—or even worse, not caring about our finances at all—it sends a clear message. Money.CNN.com recently posted an article entitled, "Kids and Money." One paragraph in particular stuck out to me:

"Long before most children can add or subtract, they become aware of the concept of money. Any 4-year-old knows where their parents get money—the ATM, of course. Understanding that parents must work for their money requires a more mature mind, and even then, the learning process has its wrinkles."

Are you handling your children's finances like an ATM? If they ask, do they receive? If you answered "Yes" to both these questions, it might be time to practice some tough financial love. The way we speak of money in our daily lives has a dramatic effect on the healthy patterns of spending and saving in our children's futures.

The first step to help your children understand the importance of money is to practice exactly what you are going to teach them, every day. Here are three key tips to helping your children understand smart money choices:

1. When shopping, make your children part of the decision process. Sometimes when shopping, we fill our carts without even thinking. I often hear from my friends that Target is one of the hardest stores to walk into and leave without overspending. Their clean aisles, great lighting and product displays are legendary for capturing our attention and dollars. The next time you walk into a store tell your child, "Mom is coming here for FIVE things. Will you help me count and mark off the things on our list?"

They'll remind you to hold yourself accountable, and you might have fun in the process.

2. Start a Spend, Save and Donate plan for birthdays and holidays. Whenever my children receive a check or cash for a birthday or celebration, we break down the money into three categories. First, we save some of the money for college or the future. Then we sometimes invest or donate a part of the money to an organization we've chosen. Lastly, we take a percentage for spending and enjoying.

3. A few times a year, go through your children's items and teach them about donating to those less fortunate. If your family is anything like mine, the holidays are a time of great spoiling and love. I try to teach my children about those that aren't as fortunate as we are by donating items every year to the Adopt a Family program with Cornerstone. We also go through our home regularly and give what we can. Most items that are in good condition can be donated, even old electronics. Visit WhereCanIDonate.com to find out more about nonprofits that will take your gently-used items.

Women and Math

Are girls really more geared towards the language arts than mathematics? A 2009 LiveScience Article explained that in countries where a larger gender equality gap was found, females performed worse than their male counterparts in math and science.

Girls in the United States are now taking calculus in high school at the same rate as boys, and the percentage of U.S. doctorates in the mathematical sciences awarded to women has climbed to 30 percent in the 21st century, up from 5 percent in the 1950s. However, more boys than girls are identified at the upper rungs of the mathematically gifted in the United States. The researchers say this gap is narrowing. Summers suggested that guys inherently show more variability than gals in math ability, resulting in some guys with soaring math skills. The variability, he pointed out, could account for the greater number of males with award-worthy math skills. (No woman to date has won a Fields Medal, the Nobel Prize of mathematics).[4]

To raise healthy girls, we must also understand that our culture diminishes their intellectual abilities. I often cringe when walking through department stores. You can always tell little girls' clothing from aisles away—the pinkness screams at me. I'm usually left un-amused by the sayings on t-shirts or clothing. "100% princess!" and "Too Cute!" hardly instill anything but the importance of appearance. Researchers found that we subconsciously speak to our daughters differently than our sons.

We must not forget that we are living, breathing examples to our little girls. When we cringe at balancing the checkbook, they take notice. I often wonder what the world will look like for my daughter, Gabrielle. Will she feel the same pressure as I did to marry and secure the "perfect future?" I hope that the lessons I teach her each day help elevate her self-esteem and belief that she can truly do anything she puts her mind to. Here are three ways you can teach your daughter

---

4. http://www.livescience.com/5482-girls-math-culture-skewed.html

about making strong financial decisions:

1. *Be the positive role model your daughter needs
   to see.*

When you take out the credit card during each shopping trip, your little girl will notice. If you truly pay off the card every month—don't just tell her, show her. Transparency can be difficult, especially when we're taught not to 'bother' our children with adult matters. However, this will keep you more in-check financially and she'll be confident that mom truly does know best!

Sometimes, saving money can be A LOT of fun. The next time your children want to go somewhere and spend money, plan an entire day together without spending one dollar. Give each child a chance to plan part of the day and watch how fun free can be. Not only will you create lasting memories with your children, you'll truly be teaching them the value of a dollar!

You might also find that shopping together isn't ruined by what you don't buy. When you take the time to explain your financial decisions, it gives your daughter the permission to have a dialog about her finances. You may find that she's saving her money from babysitting or chores to do something extra special. You might choose to reward her for not seeing the need for another pair of new shoes by matching her savings for college when she chooses to put extra money away. Positive reinforcement is as good for mom as it is for daughter.

2. Teach your kids about investing including stocks and bonds.

I love hosting workshops and classes to teach women about money. When I'm able to show women how they can prepare for their futures and elevate their income to last longer, I feel like I am truly doing what I am meant to do. You'll have the same feeling when you take the time to understand the stock market and make solid investment choices. The more we communicate what we know to our children, the better choices our children will make. I cannot explain how troubling I find it that women seem to know when the next sale is at a store, but have no idea how their stocks are doing in the market. Worse yet, some women claim it's *their husband's duty*! Ignorance is NOT bliss, especially since we are coming out of one of the worst recessions since the 1930's. Our daughters' educations are vital to their success. Let's not forget that the best education sometimes comes from home!

3. Don't shy away from the tough questions.

She might ask you, "Did you marry dad to be secure?" or "What if I don't want to be married?" She might even explain, "Everything would be easier if I just got married!" Reinforce in your daughter that she is smart enough and strong enough to make solid financial decisions, with or without a partner. Involve her in discussions with your husband about finances and the household budget while explaining why you pay what you do, cut what you do and the subtle nuances in-between. Seeing positive communication between husband and wife will boost her knowledge for the future and help her seek out strong character in her future mate.

The Credit Card Dilemma

Credit companies are targeting teens like never before. With the rise of identity theft, it's a confusing struggle to begin to understand if young adults should have a credit card. Here is one terrible story and one great solution.

Elise is the daughter of a prominent couple that has tried to educate her on the pitfalls of credit cards. During her sophomore year at college, Elise secretly opened a credit card to pay for miscellaneous expenses during her year, including a trip to see her long-distance boyfriend. When the bills started piling up and Elise couldn't find a way to pay more than the minimum, she knew she was in trouble.

At 20-years-old with over $3,000 of credit card debt, Elise had nowhere to turn but to her parents when the collection calls began. Thinking they would bail her out this once, she had no idea how angry they'd be. Mom and Dad had always used a credit card for dinner and clothing. Surely they'd understand! When Elise explained to her parents what happened, they were glad she came clean, but they told her that this was a very serious problem. Instead of partying on the weekends, Elise secured a part-time job to help pay down her credit card. After the card was paid off, Elise's parents took her card and she promised to never open another credit card again.

In a perfect world, Elise would have understood the seriousness of credit cards before she ever paid with plastic. Unfortunately, she wasn't thinking as she was spending and almost seriously damaged her credit history. If Elise's parents were my clients, I'd have invited them all into my office to develop a set of rules for the use of the credit card while educating and empowering Elise to make solid decisions. A little pre-work negates a lot of heartache.

Elise's story is one I see all too often. The importance of communicating with our young adults cannot be forgotten. There are discussions with our children we dread, and financial security doesn't have to be one of them. The more open you are about educating your children about money, the more open your children will be to ask you questions and get recommendations. Although we cannot control teen rebellion, we can arm young adults with wisdom and a place to discuss their concerns. Consider bringing your teenager or college student to your next meeting with your financial advisor. It might open their eyes to a world they never imagined!

Education and Planning for Their Future

The first key to understanding the differences between merely planning for your children's college fund and investing in their college fund is to know the difference between the Coverdell Education Savings Account and the 529 Plan.

Coverdell Accounts

I highly recommend that my clients start with the Coverdell Education Savings Account. The main reason is purely financial. You are able to put away up to $2k per year, per child (until they are 18) in the account. This money needs to be used by the time your child is 30, otherwise it will be highly taxed. Additionally, since children can only have one Coverdell, I highly recommend the Coverdell for the beginning stages of planning. You have until April 15th of every year to contribute the $2k per child for the prior tax year. There is no deduction for what you put into the account, but whatever the account grows to, as long as it is used for higher education, it can be taken out tax-free. You can invest the money in anything inside the Coverdell, even an individual stock. This is great for it allows you to have an account you can accumulate money in for higher education but also can be used as a teaching tool.

529 Accounts

The best reason to have a Coverdell and a 529 plan is that although your child can only have one Coverdell, he or she may have multiple 529 plans. The flexibility-factor is incredible. We all know that in any given year we are able to "gift" up to $13k per year. With the 529 plan, you can gift $13k for 5 years all in one lump sum today. So, you could take $65k today out of your estate and put it into a 529 plan. 529 plans are used most with gift-giving and are especially prevalent among grandparents gifting money to grandchildren. This means Grandma may gift $13k a year for 5 years and Grandpa can do the same as well. So, Grandma can contribute $65k today as well as Grandpa for a total of $130k. Now, little Johnny has $130k in his 529 plan that can grow and he can use tax-free for higher education. This money is pulled out of their estate for planning reasons all at once. Remember the tax implications of taking money out of an estate—since it's considered a gift, the grandparents won't be taxed as much after they pass away.

The Roth IRA

Another great vehicle on the highway of saving for your child's education is the Roth IRA. In any given year anyone with earned income can add up to 5k a year to the Roth IRA. Consider looking into the benefits of starting a Roth IRA for a child who is working part-time in high school or college. The key here is that your child needs to have earned an income. So, if your child worked and earned $1,500.00 for the year, you can put that $1,500.00 into the Roth for them. If your child worked and made 7k for the year, they could put the maximum contribution away into the Roth IRA which is 5k. This money can grow tax-free for a first home purchase, higher education or leave in the Roth IRA for their own retirement. The Roth IRA can be invested in anything. There is no set rate of return with an IRA.

A Note About Trust Accounts

Another option is the UTMA/UGMA accounts. This is the Uniform Transfers to Minor Act or the Uniform Gift to Minors Act. These accounts are trust accounts. Trust accounts are a wonderful gift to children, but they could hurt your child's chances of receiving financial aid. Remember that 529 plans and Coverdell accounts do not hurt your children as much in the financial aid process. Whereas the UTMA/UGMA account is like having money in a checking or savings account in regards to the availability to use for school and the financial aid calculation. The other thing to be aware of is trust funds are also taxable. So, when your child is working and earns interest on these accounts, they will pay taxes and the tax will be at their parent's tax rate. Ouch! The other thing to be aware of with the UTMA/UGMA is that when the child turns 21 they can use the money for whatever they want. You have no control. Whereas the 529 plan or Coverdell needs to be used for higher education.

Mom's and Dad's, be aware that our children's new-found wisdom may humble us in the process. Mommy might not really need those new jeans, but she sure wants them! Please practice patience with your little ones as they try to practice the "Needs and Wants" game (or the other examples I've given) with you. Getting angry at them for questioning you won't help the lesson stick. It will teach them that questioning about money is the wrong thing to do and they may become fearful. Successful parenting is all about boundaries and communication. When you find that mix when speaking about finances with your children, you've really struck gold.

Divorce Dollars and Sense

*"Divorce is the psychological equivalent
of a triple coronary bypass."*

—MARY KAY BLAKELY, *American Mom*

Divorce: A Personal Story and Reflection

Sometimes, a divorce can blow open the doors of your life and create a beautiful, new future. The Saturday after my divorce trial, I put on a new pair of heels and gathered up my group of supportive friends to celebrate. In the midst of my trial and the events leading up to the divorce being finalized, I knew I needed to take a break and a breath to truly see how far I'd come. Armed with a "Just Divorced" magnet for the limo and a few glasses of wine, we celebrated letting go of the pain and guilt that had plagued me for years.

Divorce parties have recently made headlines in the New York Times and The Today Show. Suddenly, women were celebrating starting their lives anew instead of adopting kittens or crying over cookie dough. According to Christine Gallagher, author of *Divorce Party Planner,* a Divorce Party is simply "a way to mark the end of the pain and suffering that comes with divorce." Christine believes a Divorce Party is a "ritual we need to cope with any difficult life transition." For me it was an opportunity to reclaim the negative emotions and turn the situation into a positive inspiration to look back upon. It helped me find closure.

According to the Webster Dictionary, alimony is defined as "an allowance made to one spouse by the other for support pending or after legal separation or divorce." Alimony is also known as "spousal maintenance." Spousal maintenance is based on the need of one spouse and the other's ability to pay for that need. A new trend of maintenance is "manimony"— women paying for the needs of men.

In my practice over the years, I have seen numerous women that have struggled to get spousal maintenance just to help meet their basic expenses while staying at home for years to watch the kids and take care of the home. Now, the trend has shifted to some men under-earning and expecting spousal maintenance. In my opinion, if someone stays at home, takes care of the home and the kids with years of no money going to retirement accounts or building up earning potential and income, this person (male or female) could have the potential to receive spousal maintenance.

Men and women should be subject to the same laws. I'm all for equality. But, receiving spousal maintenance or asking for it just because you think you deserve it doesn't mean you could—or should—necessarily receive it. If you are going through the divorce process and are trying to figure out how much you could receive or pay in spousal maintenance, I can help you figure out that amount.

So, what to do? Develop a bulletproof budget. Your budget is extremely important, so you want to the spend time and write out all your monthly expenses. Spend time on your budget to make sure your expenses are accurate. You do not want to forget oil changes if your husband changed your oil prior to the divorce. Manimony is a new trend and I believe it is because we women are now starting to outearn men. I don't believe we women should pay manimony just because a man decides to be under-or unemployed. I would have no problem paying spousal maintenance or supporting my clients that did if the husband was a true stay-at-home dad.

I recently went through a very difficult divorce. Like most women, I never expected that divorce would happen to me. I thought I had found Prince Charming in my now ex-husband. When I was younger, I dreamed of a white picket fence and a home with a loving spouse and children. In 2004, I came to the realization that my dream wasn't going to come true, as I was battling severe emotional abuse and some physical abuse. I quietly filed paperwork to divorce my ex-husband when our volatile relationship came to a head after I became physically ill from the abusive relationship. Looking back, it's all a little hard to believe.

Maggie's Story: My friend Maggie helped throw her best friend a Divorce Party and helped illuminate a new path. Her friend's ex moved out but she had to stay in the marriage for a variety of reasons. Some of us had helped her clean before the party. We also helped her paint her bedroom. Then we bought her new sheets and towels, wine glasses, chocolates and lingerie. Just like a bridal shower, it was a fun way to have a new beginning after her feeling like she couldn't just walk away. I think the sheets were the biggest hit.

My abuse didn't happen with a sudden gush. It started as a drip and soon that drip started to expand; before I could really understand what was going on, I was ankle-deep in confusion and fear. I never imagined that I would become a statistic. According to the Domestic Violence Resource Center 1 in 4 women have experienced a form of domestic abuse.[5] Sitting in a room with other women and knowing that I was part of the 25 percent, was both humbling and maddening.

I filed the divorce papers as a crescendo to the symphony of what I had experienced. Begging me not to go through with it, my ex-husband convinced me he was truly sorry and that he would handle his emotions better. Looking back, I can see that even in that moment he was blaming me for what happened through certain words he used or the ways he minimized my emotions. Always trying to find the positive in those around me, I desperately wanted to find the positive in our marriage and save what I could at all costs. I actually stopped the proceedings and allowed my spouse to continue to harm me, all because I wanted the fairytale. I truly believed he changed. He changed enough to satisfy me for a short while, but not for the long-term.

If I had gone through the divorce in 2004, my life wouldn't be what it is today. I don't believe one should live life with regrets. But if I would have gone through with the divorce back then, it would have cost me a lot less money but to me it doesn't matter. I now have happiness.

In 2007, I was overjoyed to learn I was pregnant with Parker (P.J.), my first child. Being a mother has strengthened

---

5. The Centers for Disease Control and Prevention and The National Institute of Justice, Extent, Nature, and Consequences of Intimate Partner Violence, July 2000. The Commonwealth Fund, Health Concerns Across a Woman's Lifespan: 1998 Survey of Women's Health, 1999

me. At P.J.'s birth, I held him, and—just like every parent—I was instantaneously changed. But that moment doesn't define your role in motherhood as much as you think it would. It is the start of an evolution toward becoming your best self. Unfortunately, as I grew and changed into motherhood, my husband did not. His anger and violent behavior escalated. A few instances of my Prince Charming's abuse are vivid in my mind, but as time passes and the divorce settles behind me, I find myself more and more empowered to evolve past him.

In 2010, my sweet angel, Gabrielle (Gabi) was born. Always my little ham, she looks for ways to make those around her smile and I find myself giggling with her daily.

The drip that started as merely one drop had now expanded from a puddle at my ankles to a reservoir up to my knees. It was hard to push through it and see that Prince Charming had never really stopped the emotional abuse. The situation escalated when one evening after witnessing him hurt one of our children, I begged him to only hurt me. In that moment I took my mental blinders off and faced a very hard decision.

My Prince Charming wasn't going to change and I needed to find hope for my children and my future. In 2010, after years of emotional and physical abuse, our divorce started. I watched my children live in fear for far too long. I made a very painful, but incredibly powerful decision to take back control of my life as my own and protect my family. When I looked back on the situation and read through pages and pages of notes that I've kept, I realized just how STRONG I am.

I am sharing my story with you to give you hope and help you understand that no matter the circumstances, you are not alone and your safety and health are far too important to negotiate.

Sara Bareilles has long-been a favorite recording artist of mine. If you've heard her song, "King of Anything," it might change your life as it has changed mine. In 2011, I ran a 5k while listening to her powerful words in cadence with the beat of my feet stepping down on the pavement. To some, it might have been just another run, but to me it was a race to freedom.

This, among many other reasons, is exactly why I wrote this book. At the end of this book, you'll find resources and tips to get out of an unhealthy relationship with your finances and emotional wellbeing intact. If you suspect that a friend is being abused, please speak up. While at first the reality may be too painful for her, your words can make all the difference in the world. Each day is a new day and it's never too late to secure a happy and safe future.

How did I get through it? I have some colorful memories of magnificent crying fests, but I also made a list of the things I just couldn't do without.

I rewrote my bucket list. Instead of focusing on what I hadn't yet accomplished, I focused on doing one thing every month. I learned a magic trick, went skydiving, kiteboarding, kayaking, drove a race car, went paddleboarding, and ran that 5k to Sarah's music. I even flew an airplane. It was never about getting back at my Prince Charming to show him I could do these things. It was simply for me—to show myself that I could stretch and grow and accomplish more than I ever dreamed.

I spent time with my friends and family. Often. Everyone needs a support group. The time to build your support group, just like your wealth, is when you don't need it. Since I was blessed with people that loved and cared about me, I was able to open up emotionally and detoxify my life.

One of my friends is a fantastic comedian. His humor and wit helped me through the darkest moments of my grief and anger. I quickly learned that a major life event truly separates the false from the real. I learned who was authentic and who was pretending. In the end, I was blessed more than I could ever imagine.

I allowed myself to feel. After years of pushing my emotions away and hiding the negative, I embraced what's happened and found the positive. They call it a "silver lining" for a reason. Sometimes, we're so busy staring at the big cloud that we forget what is on the outside. Staring at anything (especially the negative) for too long can damage us internally. I know that I control my choices and my happiness, and just knowing that I can feel is an amazing gift I've given myself.

I hired the right people. My attorney and therapist came highly recommended. I did my homework and found the right professionals for my situation and personality. Friends are meant to lean on and be there for you, but having a therapist to simply listen made a huge difference in my thought process and attitude.

I took a break. One commitment I made to myself was to get a weekly massage. Not only did I look forward to the moment when I was able to lay down and let all the week's problems float away, I was able to take the opportunity to literally get the weight of the world off my shoulders. In finding "me time," I recovered sooner from the negativity and was able to be more successful for my clients and, most importantly, a better mom to my children.

I learned to be comfortable being alone. The big turning point for me was when I was separated from my ex for over a year. In my house, I repainted the once white and stark rooms with warm, earthly shades. I even drove the boat alone and started entertaining friends and family more. I realized how isolated and disconnected I had been from those I cared about. When I took my home into my own hands, I felt that I could do anything.

Deb Schanilec is a relationship expert, specializing in helping divorced women emancipate themselves from relationship deja vu. Deb has helped countless women through end-of-relationship emotions. When we spoke recently she gave me some powerful advice:

"I remember more than 20 years ago the day I drove up Interstate 26 to get out of Hurricane Hugo's way, perfect blue skies with not a cloud in sight, only to have it follow me up the interstate that evening in all its terrifying power and majesty. I was in the middle of moving, one-third of my stuff in the old place, one-third in the new, and one-third, the really irreplaceable stuff with me in my car. I figured at least some of it would survive. And all of it did. Dwell in possibility."—Deb Schanilec

"From the moment we are born, there are facets and layers in the culture that fight against our idea of self. We are burdened with layers of meaning that others demand we recognize and buy into. What is truly important is to reconnect with what makes you happy. One exercise I do with each client is to have them write 'It's not true' on a post-it note. I have them put the note on a mirror or a place they look often. We are who we want to be and we cannot let others rule our psyche."

Here are Deb's three steps to positive emotional health after a divorce at the end of a meaningful relationship:

1. Seek out the quality of information and relationships that you need. You need a daily reminder either by phone call, email or text. Allow yourself to be open to the positivity.

2. Be willing to get together in-person with girlfriends who support you. Your network is an important tool, maximize your solid relationships to keep you steady in uncertain times.

3. Do purposeful activities. Watch movies with a positive ending. Listen to songs that have a good message.

Deb recommends that her clients look for inspiration using as many senses as possible. Inspiration can be found with smell, taste, touch and thought. Some of her favorite movies include, *Life Is Beautiful*, *Groundhog Day* and *The Shawshank Redemption*. Just like my Sarah Bareilles addiction, Deb enjoys music that makes her think, feel and dance.

Something that she said in particular got me thinking. Deb suggested I go to my favorite store and peruse the perfume counter and find a scent that speaks to me. By trying something new and changing my routine, I could program myself to see differences and think more positively.

Does it really work? Deb said that a just a few months ago a client came to her office that was struggling with bitterness from a 25-year-old divorce. Her client had been stewing in resentment and didn't recognize the value of shifting her mindset. After a few sessions and realizing the power of positive thinking, Deb's client was handed a dream job at a company she had always wanted to work for. When you discover the value of letting go of the negative and letting in the positive, great things happen.

Now that we have the positive thinking and the hope

that happiness IS out there, let's talk about the financial implications of divorce. After years in this industry, I've seen the damage of believing financial myths behind divorce or separation firsthand. The average divorce in the United States costs over $20,000. If the divorce is highly-contested, it can amount to as much as a mortgage.

No one enters into a marriage assuming they'll be divorced. We often forget about planning for our financial future in the emotional turmoil and anger of separating from our spouse. In this chapter, we'll break down popular myths behind divorce and money, and look at a few success stories.

Women need to protect themselves, especially in divorce. The best piece of advice I can give you is to find a financial advisor and determine your marital net-worth. By having an advisor as a part of the process, you'll be able to better separate your emotions from your finances. In all reality, it is JUST a car and JUST jewelry. Nothing is worth your sense of peace and emotional state. When you begin to look at your assets for their face value, you'll realize that YOU are far more important than anything on a shelf.

Over the years, I have helped many clients prepare and preserve their finances through divorce proceedings. One woman in particular, Kim, reminds me of how a situation can change depending on who you consult.

Kim hired me and we started meeting a few months before she filed for divorce. During our initial meetings, Kim explained that her ex-husband, Sam, was recently laid-off due to alcohol/drug issues on the job. Kim was a homemaker their whole marriage. Over the recent months, Sam had stopped paying the mortgage.

Upon meeting with Kim and finding her marital net worth, we came to the agreement that a divorce was needed to regain a healthy financial and mental future. Kim needed the process to be as quick and simple as possible while still understanding exactly what was at stake. Since Sam had issues with alcohol and drugs, we knew that Kim needed to start preparing for a much different life than she was used to.

Our first step was to regain control of Kim's assets to help her financial wellbeing. Sam had been cashing in the retirement accounts. Had we let the divorce proceedings continue at the normal rate, there would have been nothing left for Kim to draw from after the divorce. The worst-case scenario was that Kim would be left with no retirement savings, no house and no money to start over.

Our second step was to connect Kim with an attorney she trusted and start truly looking at her budget. We found a way to keep Kim in her home if she could land a job. By pushing the process along as fast as possible to preserve the retirement dollars, we succeeded in a few ways. Kim now has a job meeting her own expenses and has retirement money saved. It could have been an ugly divorce and an even uglier bankruptcy. Kim knew that she needed a team to work with her and empower her to change the outlook of her financial future.

This brings up one important question. Clients often ask me, "Is

Attorney Rob Hill from Larkin-Hoffman LLP, states the key to protecting yourself in the divorce process is to get involved with the situation instead of disconnecting. If children are a part of the divorce, focus your energy into being the most involved parent you can be and start educating yourself about what you owe and what you own. Instead of skimming the Internet for an attorney, ask a friend for a referral. Rob says, "Anyone can build a beautiful website. Trust your gut."

there ever a reason for a woman to just walk away?" I have a very simple answer: If you have been married for less than 3 months, have no property, mingled assets or children, you could walk away from a marriage and complete your own divorce process. Before you decide to divorce on your own, seek legal advice from a family law attorney. However, I truly believe you should never give up an asset unless you know its worth. With so many lingering questions and myths about divorce on the Internet, it's hard to know what to believe. Here are the top 5 myths about finances and divorce:

Myth #1: There is no way to save money in a divorce.

Sometimes, all you need is to do a little legwork to save money. Once you decide on an attorney for your divorce, consider taking on a lot of the preparation work yourself. Not only will you save fees with your lawyer, you'll feel more empowered about the process, your financial health and your stake in the divorce. You can save money by doing the pre-work and research yourself.

The Guide to Saving Money in Your Divorce

1. Ask for an itemized list from your attorney of what you'll need to provide. Typically the attorney representing you will want all financial documentation, i.e., loans, bank records, tax returns, plus the value of your current accounts. Check off the list each time you gather the information. Purchase an expandable folder or banker's box and keep a separate record of your financial history over the past few years. You

can label each folder by year and then sub-folder with "Car" or "Taxes." If you need help finding the value of your car, use www.kbb.com and follow the steps to locate the make, model and year. Simply print out the page with your car's details and value then tuck this information into the "Car" folder. Put one copy in your box and one in the box for your attorney. By educating yourself on the worth of your assets you'll feel better instantly, and save time and money with your lawyer at the same time.

Pro Tip:
When asking for the mortgage payoff information, make sure to get the payoff balance and the principal balance. The payoff balance will include any pre-payment charges required to satisfy the loan as well as additional months' interest. The principal balance merely represents the amount of money that needs to be paid off. To find out about any additional liens when determining the equity of your home, consider visiting the local county recorder's office. They can help you determine if any other liens are on your property and get the most up-to-date information on your home.

2. Hire a Certified Divorce Financial Analyst (CDFA). You could spend $2,000 hiring a CDFA, but this person could save you that money by giving you a single tip. A CDFA is a financial advisor that knows and understands the divorce process. They can help you develop your budget and your balance sheet (a list of your assets and liabilities), figure out child support

and spousal maintenance, determine what assets you should take as part of the divorce and help you invest your money to plan for you future.

3. Call your realtor. Often when you provide documentation to your attorney about your financial aspects, you'll also need to provide a market analysis of your home. Have a licensed realtor who you trust come to the house and conduct a competitive market analysis (CMA). Most realtors will provide this for free. A CMA typically involves a few steps. First, your home will be inspected for normal wear, tear and any underlining issues. Your neighborhood will also be analyzed for the inventory of unsold homes, location and housing data, how long they've been for sale and the average price of each home. If you'd like a more in-depth analysis, you could hire an appraiser. Before you consider having your home appraised, consult your attorney and financial advisor since the price of an average appraisal is money you may not have to spend.

Pro Tip: Never be afraid to get a second opinion. Have a realtor you trust provide the CMA. However, make sure to get a non-biased second-opinion. You'll not only be able to provide two separate views on your home's worth, but you'll feel comfortable knowing that the numbers were not adjusted.

4. Document everything you do from the moment you decide to divorce until proceedings are over. This journal can be a place to vent, find humor and deal with your emotions. Keeping good records ensures

you'll lessen the strain of having to remember what your ex-husband might have said or done and you'll have quick reference for your attorney which will save time. The average divorce takes over a year and you'll quickly tire of having to remember everything without a resource. This simple up-front step can help you save thousands of dollars.

Myth #2: You should always take the house.

Deciding whether or not to take the house or condominium during a divorce can be a very hard decision. There are many factors that should be included in your analysis. Take an assessment of your complete financial picture and look at ALL of your assets and liabilities to see if you can truly afford the house on a monthly cash-flow basis, looking at it from a long-term maintenance standpoint as well. This is something a Certified Divorce Financial Analyst can help you determine. Most of the time, women take the house because they are emotionally attached to it, but you are not stable if you struggle each month because you can't afford it.

Unsure of what to do with the house or where to even begin? Here are the basic rules of home ownership and divorce.

- If you owned the home prior to the marriage but you make the payments together after the marriage, both parties will be entitled to reimbursement for those payments. You may even be entitled to a percentage of the home's appreciation.

- Is your home the biggest asset you and your ex-husband posses? If so, you could "cash out" or "buy out" your spouse from their share with a promissory note.

- If you are awarded temporary custody during the divorce proceedings, your judge may give you the right to reside in the home during the period of separation to final divorce.

- If you are considering selling your home, remember that the home doesn't need to be sold the moment you decide to divorce. Take your time, learn about your options and then consult someone you trust.

Myth #3: Don't refinance your home!

When you take the house as part of the divorce, you want to refinance the property to get the mortgage in your own name. The first step is to check if your mortgage company will put the loan in your name without refinancing, as this could save you money. If you end up going the route of refinancing, make sure to have the other party sign a quit-claim deed.

A quitclaim deed will allow you to own the house without the other party, but allow them to remain on the mortgage. For your own protection, do not sign this document if you are not taking the house as part of the divorce. Think of it like co-signing on a car that you aren't allowed to drive. You'll be liable should the other party fail to pay the mortgage, but you have no claim to the property.

You could also do what is called a "buy out" of your home, by which you buy your ex-husband's share of the home. It's best to consult with an attorney and financial advisor to see what solution may be the most appropriate for your situation.

Myth #4: Divorce is supposed to be hard!

It's time to stop walking on eggshells. Take a moment and look at the divorce process from the standpoint of protecting yourself. Jessica is a client of mine and has always been in a very happy and successful relationship with her husband, Jim. Jim took out a student loan to finish his degree. During the same period, Jessica inherited a sum of money from a family death. Jessica wanted to take the money and pay off her husband's loans. I had a very frank conversation with Jessica, saying, "If you were ever to get divorced, you want this money to be in your own name and separate, because if the check is to you and only to you, it's not marital property."

Pro Tip: The house may not be the sticking point you think it is. When you are getting divorced and taking the house as part of the divorce, know the tax implications. The truth is there are no tax implications on the sale of the house if you have lived in the house for two of the last five years and profit no more than $250,000 as a single person or $500,000 if you sell as a married couple. If you keep the house, there are no tax consequences. Divorce is not a taxable event, but what you do with the assets from the divorce is where you could have a taxable event.

Sometimes, even when marriages are great, we have to put emotion aside and keep our financial accounts separated. Be careful not to make decisions based on emotion. Instead, educate yourself about the consequences of your financial decisions.

Myth #5: Forget about the child support. Just get out!

I have a few female clients that are getting creative and "waiving" child support. Legally, it's impossible to do. Personally, I cannot stress enough that you look at this option from all sides. I once had a client named Valerie. Valerie and her ex-husband, Paul decided against child support. Instead, Valerie decided to have Paul "chip in" when needed. For instance, Valerie's son recently needed $500 for hockey. Valerie sent Paul an email to ask him to pay half. Paul immediately sent back a reply that he had bought their child something recently, so in all fairness, he would only send $12. Imagine Valerie's surprise! Soon, to distance herself from the frustration and emotional toll, Valerie stopped asking Paul for

Pro Tip:
Look into hiring a parenting consultant as well as a Certified Divorce Financial Analyst. Parenting consultants (PC's) step in to make decisions if parents cannot or will not agree. Since PC's rarely make financial decisions, you can assemble a wonderful team to focus on your family, while others can guide you through the divorce process. Remember to make sure that the PC and the financial analyst are certified and neutral so both parties are treated with respect, no matter the situation.

money completely. If you want to waive child support, consider setting up a college education account that is funded by the other party and held by a financial advisor. This may ease your concerns, frustrations and help invest in your child's future.

You can get through this. Remember that divorce is another opportunity to create positive money memories. As dire and emotional as the situation might be, remember that you can only control yourself. By remaining steadfast in realizing your control, you release yourself from the toxic blame game. Watch as your financial future starts to grow more positive with one simple decision!

"Women negotiate their safety for the financial resources they need for their children."

—CAROL ARTHUR, DAP EXECUTIVE DIRECTOR.

The Truth About Domestic Violence

- The statistics are sobering... every 9 seconds, a woman is battered in the U.S. (*Family Violence Prevention Fund, 1994.)*

- 95 percent of all victims of domestic violence are women. (*Bureau of Justice Statistics Special Report, U.S. Dept. of Justice.)*

- Domestic Violence is the single major cause of injury to women, more than muggings and car accidents combined. *(First Comprehensive National Health Study of American Women, The Commonwealth Fund, 1993.)*

- Domestic Violence is the cause of 30 percent of physical disabilities in women. (*California Department of Social Services, 1994.*

As an avid advocate for women seeking financial freedom and security, I have supported not only my clients, but prospective clients through domestic abuse. What we often fail to realize is that domestic abuse touches every aspect of a woman's life. Not only can a woman be isolated from friends and family, but her own finances as well. I once had a client that started writing out checks for $20 over the amount of her original purchase at the checkout to save money to exit her unhealthy relationship.

"Financial abuse happens over a long period of time.
You may not even notice it happening.
Be empowered and know who has access and what names
are associated with your accounts."
—Nicole N. Middendorf, CDFA

My main goal is to empower women with solid financial advice. For those affected by domestic violence, please remember three key tips:

1. Remember that any type of abuse, whether physical, mental, emotional or financial, is never your fault and there are resources that can help you. If you feel you might be in an unhealthy relationship, please reach out to someone you trust or call one of the numbers I have provided at the end of the book. Your safety and health is far too important to put off in fear that someone might not take you seriously. Asking for help takes profound courage.

2. Know whose name your titles, bills, bank accounts and investments are in. Always try to maintain an IRA in your own name with your own financial advisor. Your knowledge is power and sitting down with your financial advisor will help you regain confidence and a different outlook on your money. Don't forget that you can find a financial advisor that will meet with you for free. Yes, you want to have YOUR OWN financial advisor, someone that is there as an advocate for you.

3. Keep cash on hand for emergencies. I generally recommend enough to last you a couple of months, should you have to move immediately. Keep this account stashed away somewhere safe. You also want to have your own checking and savings account that is separate and secret.

I recently sat down with Caroline Cox, owner of LittlePinkBook.com. Cited as America's #1 resource for working women, Caroline delivers career strategy, insight and solid advice to inspire women to find greater success at work. Caroline and I discussed the most important financial aspect of domestic abuse.

Nicole: We talk so much about domestic violence, but we often glaze-over the financial aspects. How can we change this?

Caroline: Women are finally gaining more control and feeling empowered about money. In domestic abuse cases, the woman has so much work to do emotionally to get healthy, the topic of financial security is often pushed to the wayside. We know that controlling someone with money is another form of abuse. Confidence is one of the things I believe abusers take from women. The number one way to avoid losing financial control in abusive situations is to have checking, savings, IRA, 401(k) and assets in your name.

Planning for Success

*"Even when you think you have your life all mapped out,
things happen that shape your destiny in ways you might
never have imagined."*

—DEEPAK CHOPRA

Planning for the Future: Why it Matters

I want to share with you a very scary statistic. According to a recent study commissioned by the Transamerica Center, only 8 percent of working American women believe that they're committing enough to their retirement savings. Nearly one third of the women surveyed claim to "never" talk about the subject around friends and family. Are some of us scared or embarrassed?

I think it's a combination of three things: fear, ignorance and laziness. Ouch, right? Some of us assume our partners will take care of retirement, while others are finding it hard to put away ANY money towards retirement. With most of America living paycheck to paycheck, retirement is all-too-often an afterthought in the financial planning process.

The prospect of trying to save money in a time of economic turmoil isn't at the forefront of women's minds. Every dollar counts in the current market, so it's understandable why women begin to shy away from saving, let alone saving for their retirement. They have car payments, student loans, rent, mortgages, school fees, insurance payments and monthly bills. Two-thirds of women are working jobs that pay less than $30,000 per year. Almost half of that same two thirds work those jobs without 401(k) or other retirement plans. How are they supposed to protect themselves moving forward when they're just trying to get through today?

As a society, we work throughout our lives with the purpose and intention of providing for ourselves and our loved ones. We put in our time trying to earn the privilege of receiving the chance to walk away from the workplace on our terms. These terms generally mean certain sacrifices will be made during the length of a career. Every vacation or car that was attainable was instead pushed aside for another luxury. Although it manifests itself differently for everyone, retirement represents the reward for responsibility. It truly affords one the life they would prefer to lead outside of work. For men and women, retirement means different things.

Men want to be financially comfortable when they eventually step away from a career. Fiscal confidence means a great deal to women, but they focus on the things money can't buy instead.

Associated expenses might simply be the costs of pursing the activities you love or the expenses of fulfilling your dreams. They also may have to deal with the uncertainty of outliving a spouse or partner and facing the world alone. Women, on average, live longer than men, meaning their resources will have to outlast a man's too. Some women will be lucky enough to inherit some of their deceased husband's savings. The truth is, the world is changing and we ALL need to focus on saving, growing and keeping our assets, no matter our marital status.

In the financial process, each one of us needs help in attaining new levels of understanding. Although I consider myself an expert on retirement, savings and investments, I am constantly learning about human behavior and how I can best help my clients. Discussing monetary goals, fears and shortcomings can give women a better foothold on their ability to make the best decisions. Those decisions will lead to greater confidence, and greater confidence means happier women!

Fifty-seven percent of American women aged 65 or older are single. These women are saddled with making difficult decisions by themselves, which is a harrowing prospect for anyone who is ill-informed. Over the years, the level of Social Security protection for women has been strengthened, but we are unaware of what might happen with the program.

As Social Security becomes an even more volatile issue in the U.S., we should be aware that nearly 60 percent of those receiving Social Security are women. Many of the Baby Boomers who have retired or are set to retire have long-planned on using the funds provided from Social Security as their main source of income, which is a terrible idea. Social Security is a tax, plain and simple. It's not meant to be retirement savings and surely, it's not meant to be counted on.

Save your funds in a 401(k) or IRA. It's never too late. As the Social Security system has become compromised and drained, the amount of money citizens contributed may not match the expected payout they anticipate. This leaves many women sadly stuck. While the government and powers that be are currently grappling over what's next for Social

Security, generations still working should see this issue as greater incentive to think about their retirement.[6]

Before women will be able to start investing in stocks, bonds, money-market accounts and various other investment options, they must first be secure enough to part with capital. This starts with saving money early and keeping up-to-date with your plan. If you were to create a roadmap for this process, it might look a bit like this:

1. **Fuel up the car.** Understand where your finances sit today, at this moment, and pick up the phone to call a financial advisor. With your help, we're the fuel that can make your car go faster without getting lost or stuck at the side of the road in the process.

2. **Set up a plan.** With help from a professional, set a reasonable number and calculate how much money you would need to stow away on a monthly basis to reach that goal (based on current salary).

3. **Go, baby, go!** Begin to schedule out how you will "pay yourself" from your salary. A concrete agenda in your mind will make you more likely to continually place money aside every month. Pull money automatically from your checking or savings to an investment account or your IRA. This also eliminates the "I forgot to this time" excuse. You'll also be less likely to cheat yourself if you're not the one physically removing money from an account.

The more you remove "you," the greater the chance of success. Remember, this money will be the beginnings of your life after work. This is YOUR plan for success.

---

6. http://www.ssa.gov/pubs/10127.html#a0=0

The Importance of Education

Every parent wants to see their children graduate and live the best lives possible. While time always seems to go by more quickly than we think, our retirement needs to come before our children's college fund. A financial advisor can help you find the right savings-ratio for securing a future for yourself and your not-so-little ones.

Teenagers intent on attending post-secondary institutions can achieve and/or receive scholarships, grants and loans to help shoulder the initial costs. Retirement doesn't afford any of these relievers. This is an arena where women should really consider their own futures as they often do with their children. Think of it as a lesson in tough love: mothers may help their children when and/or if they're able.

Don't become reliant on Social Security. Here are three tips to keep you financially independent:

1. Take responsibility for your future and fund your own pension. We can no longer rely on companies or the government to fund our future. Our success lies in our own hands.

2. Chat with a financial advisor about maximizing your own 401(k) and IRA.

3. Ask yourself difficult questions. Is it time to downgrade to a less expensive house? By formulating a plan, we can cut unnecessary expenses.

Way to Go, Mom!

A client of mine is a single mother. In discussing finances with her daughter early, she decided to bring her teenager in to see me. Mom was able to take advantage of tax benefit retirement accounts and matched her daughter's savings money to help her get started. Now at

18, her daughter has a Roth IRA and great saving and spending habits. Way to go, Mom!

Investing 101

Women are traditionally more frugal and wary when it comes to investing. Understanding how to improve your chances of making your money work for you takes effort. Start to educate yourself by asking questions, learning the jargon and knowing the historical pitfalls. Question your employer about the intricacies of your 401(k) plan, IRA, 403(b) or 457 plan and how you can better understand their impact. How much will it cost you in the short-term to make catch-up contributions?

Read up and keep tabs on the traditional financial powerhouses like The Wall Street Journal, Forbes, Fortune and Bloomberg News. The financial industry doesn't have to seem like another language. You are smart enough and determined enough to educate yourself with how investing and the stock market works. By simply having an understanding of the industry, you'll find some of the fear of investing is gone! After all that, what is the difference and how do they affect a woman's financial goals? Start with the two basics: stocks and bonds.

Stocks or Bonds?

A stock is defined by Stanford as partial ownership of a company. When larger companies start seeking additional funding for their potential enterprise, they often go beyond private investments. This public ownership affords certain voting rights based on the amount of stock a shareholder possesses. A bond is a form of debt through which you act as the bank. The longer you hold that bond, the more interest you collect on its original price.

Which option is better between stocks and bonds? Here's the tricky part: you want to have both. A diversified portfolio and money in things such as commodities, businesses, real estate and so much more could help fund your future.

Should I Purchase Stock?

Before you make any large purchase, you need to truly understand what you are buying. For stocks, we look at the potential of a company or product. If you believe the company has sound strategy, a reliable product and is on its way to becoming the next Apple (and I'm not saying you should buy or sell Apple stock), stock is the better choice. Stock makes the company's successes your successes. In the same fashion, the business' failings will affect you as well. It's best to think of stock as a partnership.

Some bonds are like investing in a Certificate of Deposit (CD). For example, Treasury Notes could be compared to CD's but of course corporate bonds could not. You know that whatever monies you were promised in the future will not change, regardless of success or failure if you hold the bond (or CD) to maturity. Your investment does not allow you any say in the company or institution's workings; it only guarantees the return of your original funding, plus interest. In the end, stocks and bonds have been around for a long time and are traditionally a wiser choice for trigger-shy investors as long as you have a diversified portfolio and are investing for the long term. As with any investing, there is potential for loss, so seek out personalized advice from a financial advisor to understand your specific situation.

I Still Don't Understand...

A stock is me, the author of the book. I own Prosperwell Financial which is my own company. If I was open to other shareholders or was a publically traded company you could give me money and own stock or shares in my company. As my company grows as a shareholder you could gain value. It is my company and what I do everyday. Or think of it like this, you can buy my book and invest in my message. Whereas, a bond is a loan, like a mortgage or car payment.

Life Insurance

Life insurance is also a very popular retirement idea pinned on women and is oftentimes sold as an investment. Let's all repeat together: *"Insurance is not an investment!"* Though some may use the word "investment," they are merely selling peace of mind.

The appeal of whole life insurance is the staggering returns after some deep cuts during the early years of the policy. It packages lifelong insurance and savings together. Women see the potential of saving money along with the protection of life insurance in case of their untimely death, in which case their family would hypothetically be financially secure. Life insurance agents play the cash value of the policy, which is the main reason for families to invest heavily in whole life plans. According to financial director Dave Ramsey, whole life policies aren't worth the hype and never bring home the full value the policyholder intended.

SmartMoney.com positions whole life insurance as the more expensive, less productive of the two kinds of life insurance. For those looking for the assurance and security of life insurance, term-life is the more efficient selection. With policies ranging from one to thirty years, term-life is the cheaper way to have protection for your family without the same financial handcuffing.

Realize that life insurance is not an investment. Life insurance is to protect your dependents. Women need to resist the temptation of trying to do everything on their own. You can use various investment vehicles to diversify. Mutual funds could be easier to manage because of the constant professional eye watching over those investments. But this does not mean that is what you should invest in or that it is right for you. I believe you want to pick the best of the best and have a diversified portfolio. If managing your money seems overwhelming that is where you enlist the help of a financial advisor for they can be your mentor.

With all of these investments, the obvious risk is the loss of your original funding. An issue that is not as prevalent is the ability to over commit. When something appears to be too good to be true, it's best to back away and reevaluate your options. These investments are building blocks for your future, not toys for a broker or financial advisor to throw around with abandon.

There is an art to balancing capital between each level of investing and proven ways to keep everything on track. Knowing risk profiles and assessing investment performance is like an employee background check and the return on investment in marketing. Each can be tangibly defined and explained in laymen's terms. Take a chance with what you can and/or feel comfortable with and protect and grow the rest.

"Debt is such a powerful tool, it is such a useful tool, it's much better than colonialism ever was because you can keep control without having an army, without having a whole administration."

—SUSAN GEORGE

The Crisis of Debt

To fully plan and prepare for our futures, we need to release ourselves from debt. Most people in today's economy are in debt. Whether it's student loans, medical bills, credit cards or a mortgage, we are a nation that has an unhealthy view on debt and accountability. Three out of every four Americans deal with some form of debt, with almost half in a mortgage. Forty-five percent of those Americans think that they have too much debt in relation to their income. Of those with debt, 23 percent have difficulty meeting the monthly payments on their borrowings. Considering that 50.8 percent of U.S. citizens are women (according to the 2010 Census), the female population shoulders at least half of this burden.[7]

"Females have fought for equality over the last decades," says Georgina Earle, director of Women in Debt, a debt advisement company in the United Kingdom. "We have wanted independence from our spouses and to be able to afford a lifestyle based on this equality." I couldn't agree more. While two types of debt exist (good debt and bad debt), we need to embrace planning for the future to be financially stable in our futures, instead of wanting what is around us.

I found an interesting statistic that states, "Since the beginning of the 20th century, women have fought valiantly

---

7. http://www.politico.com/static/PPM192_asr_consumer_finance_survey-full_report.html

to gain the acceptance and impartiality of their male counter-parts in the workforce. In the last 30 years, the percentage of women contributing to their family's income has risen from 26.6 percent to 37.1 percent."[8] How on earth can we focus on achieving debt-free living while functioning at our best with a society that degrades our worth? Our daily lives are split between work, family, friends and, for some, school. These fractions of each day begin to take a toll on our pockets and our emotional stability.

Manisha Thakor is a personal financial expert that focuses on women. The mission statement on her website claims that, "While personal finance is important for both genders, it is extra important for us as women." Thakor comes from the same school of thought as I. Women live longer, earn less and spend 11½ years less in the paid workforce than men. Thakor calls this the 77/11 Effect.

Thakor's 77/11 Effect is a simple way to illustrate the $0.77 on the dollar women earn compared to men, and the 11 years they spend outside of the paid workforce. The Effect also factors in the five extra years that women outlive men on average, according to the CDC. All three of these issues contribute significantly to why women cannot readily pay back the debt they have accrued.

The loans they amass do not come with any discount, unlike the wages they earn. In addition, women are charged higher premiums for health insurance and still have greater out-of-pocket costs for things like contraception and maternity care. The truth is, we are asked to manage a family, work a full-time job and still have time to be a great wife/girlfriend

---

8. http://www.forbes.com/sites/manishathakor/2011/05/10/
    the-7711-effect-will-it-hurt-someone-you-know/)

or partner.[9] When do women get time for themselves?

Here is where women arrive at a crossroad. Women seem to be doing more right than wrong, yet the debt continues to pile higher and higher. Some problems and concerns will always be out of your hands. This is called *life*. Inflation will always cause issues for those trying to repay loans from a cheaper time. The salaries will not readily reflect the same inflated costs, making it that much more difficult. The fact is, in the financial world, unless you plan, you are set up to fail.

With all of these issues comes the stress. Women deal with stress differently than men, due primarily to the hormone oxytocin. In humans, stress causes cortisol and epinephrine to be released into the blood stream, raising blood pressure and decreasing the efficiency of the immune system. Oxytocin, found in both sexes, is meant to relax the body and is released in larger dosage in women. The three hormones produce a cocktail in women that leaves them in a situation of a confused body and, you guessed it … greater stress.

Stress also leads many people to indulge in their vices. The stereotypical anecdote about women under duress is that we will go shopping to relieve their angst. Is there any truth to this cliché?

While a new pair of shoes may alleviate or ease some of the pain of a rough day, many women are forgoing the mall in an effort to be more aware of their spending habits. This is a very good thing. It's reported that 18 percent of women now actively consult financial advisors. I want to state this number again because I think it's a staggering view to how many women are currently on earth: EIGHTEEN PERCENT! As a financial advisor, I am not a credit counselor.

---

9. http://www.time.com/time/specials/packages/
   article/0,28804,1930277_1930145_1930309,00.html)

Many women wait until they are far over their heads in debt to call me, or any other professional. This is one of the worst mistakes you can make.

A couple recently consulted me for financial advice. They were living way beyond their means. Even though they had various goals (in addition to retiring), if they kept spending at their usual rate, they might've ended up homeless. In sitting down and discussing their lifelong dream, we found a way to focus on one, singular goal: to buy a boat. For them, the boat was a tangible representation of all their unhappy spending. They bought clothing, travel and extra meals out all because they were unhappy that they couldn't afford the boat.

Tip:
Stop anything you are doing this moment (even reading this book). Go to the kitchen. Grab a glass of water and drink. Studies show the more water our bodies take in, the better our mood, stress level and overall health. We are no good to others if we pile on the emotional and physical weights of our lives without taking care of our bodies!

We found a way to invest in savings, to stop spending money on frivolous and unneeded expenses and the boat became possible. The most important advice I give to my clients is to simply have goals. Give yourself the gift of taking time to decide what truly matters to you and write it down in a place you see daily, then have a financial advisor that will hold you accountable.

To succeed in the financial world, you need to have an understanding of cash flow. Saving versus spending is the yin and yang of fiscal peace. Need weighs heavily against available resources, calling tough decisions on what to purchase and what to pass on. Women want their long-term goals to be understood by others, and most importantly by themselves. One solution I can offer is to start saving NOW. The more that is saved early, less needs to be contributed later. It's so simple, but it's harder than it sounds. To those starting out, here are a few ways to begin chipping away at—perhaps even preventing—debt:

Live Within Your Means. It's rhetoric by now, but those who live within their means successfully don't need to worry about financial woes as time passes. Those who have mastered this kind of philosophy rarely use credit or debit cards, paying the majority of their expenses in cash. Using cash for more purchases makes it easier to track what you're spending and how it's spent. Cash will force you to reevaluate which purchases are absolutely essential and which are luxuries. You can't spend what you don't have. The luxuries you can always look forward to give you something to work towards. Eliminate extra credit cards while keeping one for emergencies. If you try in earnest to only use cash, you'll be surprised how much unnecessary debt you can shed.

Rent or Buy? Living within your means will also force you to evaluate what kind lifestyle you have (or would like to have). If your career forces you to travel a lot, it's probably not a great idea to buy a house, though each situation is different. Renting gives you the flexibility to jump from lease to lease while only losing what you agreed to with the landlord. On the other side of the coin, if you're ready to settle down in one place, a house to call home is the best investment. Remember, bigger is not better. A starter home sometimes tells a better and more comforting story about your level of responsibility. The truth is, you don't need the mansion. As we've learned in the other chapters, that mansion won't satisfy your unhappiness.

Match the Education Costs. Generation Y thought it would be alright to go to (or back to) college and pursue a degree in whatever you wanted at the university of your dreams. The banks also salivated at the vision of you changing your major three times after your junior year based on your indecision.

Women are now the majority of students on college campuses, an achievement that was hard fought. As with any student, do your best to evaluate every career option in regards to your skill set. Don't focus on the title of the degree; instead hone in what careers are available that genuinely pique your interest. Ask questions of industry professionals, they'll be happy to discuss their career choice and responsibilities.

A college education is expensive, so in the same vein of doing homework on careers, be sure to understand the cost of each prospective school. Some schools are able to charge based on their brand in collegiate athletics. If you're not swayed by big Ivy League schools, try to stay close to home and seek out every grant that you're eligible for. In short, see to it that your tuition doesn't force you to seek out huge loans. The loans will follow you just as far your degree if they're that prominent.

Consider Credit Counseling. Quick fixes, such as dipping into your 401(k) or home equity can seriously harm your future stability. In the heat of the moment at 2 a.m., you may be tempted to think of more creative solutions, like pawning gold or a payday loan to achieve peace from debt. The problem is, each one of these solutions is a short-term fix with long-term problems.

You may get in over your head in a vicious cycle. Some debt collectors will tell you to utilize ANY resources you have, including the four given above.

Remember, credit never fixes a situation, it simply makes the situation manageable. Tapping out assets will not stabilize your finances. When a collector calls, you have a resource that is often forgotten. Call a credit counselor, just like Tara McCarthy from Financial Rehabilitation, Inc. Tara recently sat with me and discussed four questions you need to answer when you call a credit counselor:

1. Are they 501(c) certified? Find out if whomever you are calling is a nonprofit company and one that doesn't make money from your financial trouble.

2. Do they have accreditation from the ASFE? Accreditation is important and can mean the difference between speaking with a qualified professional and one that shouldn't be picking up the phone.

3. Are they approved by the HUD Department of Justice? Be aware of who you are talking with and make sure they have the needed credentials and resources.

4. Are you ready to let go of the shame or fear and find a solution TODAY? You can't be ashamed of your situation if you're going to actively change your life. It's time to let go of the negativity. Arm yourself with a partner to manage your debt and create your own path to financial wellness. You need to talk about your credit, whether you want to or not.

Plan for Big and Emergency Purchases. Thirty percent of your credit score is attached to your debt. Your credit score is simply a level of a risk that banks and financial institutions use to calculate your payments.

The best time to ask for money is when you don't need

money. When you are financially secure, start thinking about getting approval for a loan or creating an emergency fund. We all set aside money for the vacation of a lifetime. It's tangible and exciting. There is a date that can be looked forward to, a circled event on the calendar. That vacation is a want, something we've always thought about being able to do for ourselves or our families. It's a treat for all. Emergencies are a bit abstract in comparison. They're also just as much of a want to be able to cover in all circumstances.

Hypothetically speaking, say you're forced out of work for a few months due to a physical injury. How would you cover that lost income? Where would the money come from when it was needed most? Planning for these unexpected costs is very difficult and we tend try not to think in such negatives. Women worry more than men, which may allow us to think about and prepare for the worst. Set aside a separate account for this emergency fund, preferably away from your savings account that you may tap into. This will lead to less temptation to blend the two accounts on a day when you feel immortal.

Know Your Rights. The Fair Debt Collection Practices Act states that you are entitled to be treated with true fairness, dignity and respect. Swearing, threatening legal action, calling repeatedly and calling third parties are all illegal practices some debt collectors use to scare you into paying debt. Whether it's medical debt, consumer debt or school loans, talk to the billing department to set up a payment arrangement and hit those payments within 30 days. If you are more than 30 days past due with no plan, consider calling a credit counselor like Tara. The state of your financial future depends on what you do today!

Women of the 21st century have more on their plate

77

than any other time in history. They are required to spread their time and talents across many channels, leaving them deficient in certain areas. Not everyone is perfect, yet every now and then we catch ourselves trying to model what is so often showcased on the pages of a magazine. What inspires me most is when a client looks across the table from me and says, "I get it now." The best step you can take to protect yourself in ANY part of the debt process is to arm yourself with professionals to help.

Planning For the Future: Why Legal Documents Matter

You may think planning for the future is pure optimism, but I know from my own experience and what I've seen with my clients, it's purely necessary. To really understand why you need to plan ahead, we must remember that our lives are an unfinished book. While we know what has already occurred, we have no idea what will yet happen. By planning both for protecting the assets you already have and future gain, you'll have a well-rounded succession plan that will eliminate doubt and help you reach your financial goals.

Most of the time, financial planning includes making an entire life plan, for this reason alone I highly suggest having a will or health-care directive and a power-of-attorney document. Let's breakdown each one and find out why they are important.

Will or Trust

You've seen the movies where a family of a rich, deceased older man or woman sits around the table and bickers over the estate. Sadly, that happens more than you could ever imagine, (and not just for the wealthy!). A will or trust is absolutely vital in anyone's financial planning.

A will is a binding legal document that leaves zero guesswork to who inherits your estate after you pass on. According to the USA Today, only 71% of Americans have wills currently in place. There are three important questions wills answer:

1. Who receives your financial estate when you die?

2. Who receives your property (house, items within your home, etc)?

3. Most importantly, who will be the guardian of your children, should you die prematurely?

A will spells out many things including how your estate, (financial and tangible) is divided up. It also discusses your debt like mortgages and loans. There are many commercials that offer free or cheap wills by simply filling out the forms online. A will needs to be legally submitted and held by an attorney. It's far too important of a piece of paper and process for it to be done incorrectly. I've had Estate Planning Attorneys tell me they would rather you have nothing than to have something that is wrong and not specific to your state.

Most importantly, your will needs to be kept in a place that is secure, but is not secret. Our family needs to know you have a will in place and where it is located, (which attorney, where in the house, etc.) Please speak with an estate planning attorney and your financial advisor to find out more about how to file a will. Ideally, you already have a will in place, but if you are one of the 71%, it's time to start taking planning seriously.

The most important thing you can ever do for your kids, is to make a plan should something happen where you cannot care for them.

Health-Care Directives

A health-care directive is a legal form that is filed with your attorney stating who can make decisions for you legally regarding medical issues if you are unable to. It is much more than the "do not resuscitate" document that is often spoken about. Each state handles health-care directives differently, so it's vital you discuss your state's laws with an attorney. According to health.state.mn.us your health-care directive must have the following to be legal: Your directive must be dated and in writing, it must also state your name and be signed by yourself and someone you authorize to sign the form. Your signature must be verified by a notary or two witnesses. Most importantly it must include the appointment of an individual that is authorized to make health care decisions for you and/or instructions about the health care choices you wish to make.

Power of Attorney (POA)

Just like a health-care directive protects you in medical situations, a power of attorney, protects you in life's situations. The first type of power of attorney is a durable power of attorney, or DPOA. This allows you to give another individual the legal authority to make decisions for you in any setting. In fact, you can have multiple DPOA's for different situations or settings. If you become incapacitated, the DPOA is still in effect, until a general power of attorney. There are also two types of DPOA's: onging or springing. Ongoing DPOA's are in effect in any situation, without changes with the same individual. Springing DPOA's only go into effect in certain situations. One example would be if you were suddenly in a coma or incapacitated and needed someone to make decisions for you. Speak with your financial advisor and estate planning attorney to delegate whom you might want acting on your behalf for one of life's many situations.

It is important to take care of yourself and protect your assets. I will leave you with this analogy. When you are on a plane, what do they tell you to do? If something happens put the air mask on yourself first, then to assist the person next to you. So take care of yourself and see an estate planning attorney so you can take care of those around you.

Resources

www.Prosperwell.com

Prosperwell Financial has many tools available to help you with your money. Please visit the website to find our budget worksheet, divorce checklist, articles and information, or to sign up for our free newsletter.

www.childrenanddivorce.com/

Divorce resource for parents, professionals and children addressing questions asked about divorce by parents, doctors, nurses, teachers, psychologists, social workers and more.

www.divorceonline.com/

Divorce Online provides free articles and information on financial, legal, psychological, real-estate and other aspects of divorce.

www.alwaysfamilycenter.com

Great resource for people that are dealing with family conflict.

www.collaborativelaw.org

Inter-disciplinary approach to dispute resolution, drawing on the skills of professionals in the fields of law, mediation, financial analysis and mental health.

www.cooperativepracticenetwork.com

Cooperative practice is a flexible, confidential process where the parties work together to resolve their differences actively assisted by lawyers, who use a variety negotiation techniques and strategies.

www.domesticabuseproject.com

DAP promotes safe and healthy family relationships by stopping domestic violence as it occurs and working to prevent it in the future.

www.guidingway.com

Your guiding light during life's most challenging transitions.

www.happilyeverafterall.com

Resources for women encountering divorce, infidelity and child custody issues.

www.sojournerproject.org

The organizations purpose is to increase the safety of victims of domestic violence and abuse through comprehensive services and community education.

www.tubman.org

Helping families in distress find healing.

National Domestic Violence Hotline

Staffed 24-hours-a-day by trained counselors who can provide crisis assistance and information about shelters, legal advocacy, health care centers and counseling.

1-800-799-SAFE (7233) 1-800-787-3224 (TDD)

The Rape, Abuse & Incest National Network (RAINN) is the nation's largest anti-sexual assault organization. Among its programs, RAINN created and operates the National Sexual Assault Hotline at 1.800.656.HOPE a and the National Sexual Assault *Online* Hotline (rainn.org). This nationwide partnership of more than 1,100 local rape crisis centers provides victims of sexual assault with free, confidential services, 24/7. These hotlines have helped over 1.3 million people since RAINN's founding in 1994.

Statistics:

www.census.gov/compendia/statab/cats/international_statistics.html

maritalmediation.com/2011/07/demystifying-divorce-statistics

www.divorcemag.com/statistics/statsUS.shtml

www.divorcestatistics.org/

www.aardvarc.org/dv/statistics.shtml

www.dvrc-or.org/domestic/violence/resources/C61/

www.ncadv.org/files/DomesticViolenceFactSheet(National).pdf

www.americanbar.org/groups/domestic_violence.html

www.rileycenter.org/domestic-violence-statistics.html

About the Author

Nicole N. Middendorf, CDFA is a Financial Advisor and Certified Divorce Financial Analyst with Prosperwell Financial. Nicole has been professionally trained in retirement planning for small businesses and practical investments for the general public. The strategies considered are based on each investor's goals and dreams, as well as market conditions and circumstances. **Nicole is a frequent contributor in the media, where she makes guest appearances to discuss personal finance.** Nicole focuses on education for her clients for her mission is to help individuals to successfully manage their wealth and have the confidence to be in control of their financial happiness.

Nicole graduated from St. Cloud State University in St. Cloud, Minnesota with an International Business degree. Prior to forming her own company, Prosperwell Financial, Nicole was a Financial Advisor and Retirement Planning Specialist with Morgan Stanley in Wayzata, Minnesota. Nicole now offers her clients access to a wide range of financial products through LPL Financial, which include stocks, bonds, mutual funds, exchange traded funds, asset management and insured certificates of deposit. Nicole is also licensed in Life Insurance, Fixed Annuities as well as licensed to offer Variable Annuities and Managed Futures through LPL Financial.

Nicole was born and raised in Minnetonka, Minnesota. Nicole lives in Wayzata with her son Parker Jefferson and daughter Gabrielle Rose. Nicole is active in the Eden Prairie Chamber of Commerce, Alliance for Women in Media, National Association of Women Business Owners (NAWBO), Collaborative Law Institute, Cooperative Practice Network, BestPrep, along with volunteering at Cornerstone and The Domestic Abuse Project.

In 2003, Nicole was selected as one of the 25 Women to Watch from The Business Journal, the recipient of the National Association of Women Business Owners "Woman on the Way" award, and also honored with the Woman of Achievement Award from the Twin West Chamber of Commerce. In 2004, Nicole was honored with the Outstanding Young Woman of the Year award from the Minnesota Women of Today and as Volunteer of the Year from BestPrep. In 2005, Nicole was a finalist for the Emerging Entrepreneur of the Year award from the Twin West Chamber of Commerce. In 2006, Nicole was the recipient of the National Association of Women Business Owner's Young Business Woman of the Year Award. In 2007, Nicole was the recipient of the Women of Achievement award from NAWBO and an honoree of Top Women in Finance from Finance & Commerce. In 2010, the Eden Prairie Chamber of Commerce presented Nicole with the ATHENA award. Also in 2010, Nicole was selected as an honoree of Top Women in Finance Circle of Excellence from Finance & Commerce. In 2012, Nicole was honored as one of the Business Journal's "40 Under 40". *Awards based on visibility, community activity, and service.